EXPLORER BOOKS

POLAR BEARS

AND OTHER ARCTIC ANIMALS

by
Melissa L. Kim

A TRUMPET CLUB ORIGINAL BOOK

For Richard, Penny, and the three Davids

Published by The Trumpet Club
666 Fifth Avenue, New York, New York 10103

ISBN: 0-440-84694-3

Printed in the United States of America
January 1992

3 5 7 9 10 8 6 4 2
CWO

PHOTOGRAPH CREDITS

p. 31: © Comstock.   *p. 32: top,* © Dan Guravich/Photo Researchers, Inc.; *bottom,*
© G.C. Kelley/Photo Researchers, Inc.   *p. 33: top,* © Dan Guravich/Photo
Researchers, Inc.; *bottom,* © Alan Briere/SuperStock.   *p. 34: top,* © Pat Lynch/
Photo Researchers, Inc.; *bottom,* © Carleton Ray/Photo Researchers, Inc.   *p. 35:
top,* © Bill Curtsinger/Photo Researchers, Inc.; *bottom,* © Holton Collection/
SuperStock.   *p. 36: top,* © Ernest Manewal/SuperStock; *bottom,* © Tom
McHugh/Photo Researchers, Inc.   *p. 37: top,* © Leonard Lee Rue/SuperStock;
bottom, © Tom McHugh/Photo Researchers, Inc.   *p. 38:* © Fred Baldwin/Photo
Researchers, Inc.

Cover: © Mia & Klaus/SuperStock

Contents

Introduction

"The Pole at last! My dream and ambition for 23 years. Mine at last . . ."

Robert Peary wrote these words in his diary on April 6, 1909. It's no wonder he was so excited. Peary had already tried four times to do what no other modern explorer had done before—to reach the North Pole. He'd endured bitter cold, fierce competition, and crushing disappointment. He had also lost nine of his toes from frostbite!

Finally, in 1909, Peary set out with fellow American Matthew Henson and four Eskimos on the last leg of his fifth journey to the pole. Moving across a "desert of ice," the team crawled across thin ice, dragged sleds over ridges of broken ice, and walked for 10 hours a day. On April 6, Peary and Henson reached the North Pole. They raised the U.S. flag, and cheered.

Peary and Henson paved the way for the arctic exploration that followed. But they

1

weren't the first men ever to visit the Arctic. In fact, 20,000 to 30,000 years ago, primitive hunters from Asia wandered through in search of bears and foxes. The first settlers were the Inuit Eskimos, who arrived from central Asia between 6,000 and 10,000 years ago.

Explorers from Western Europe began traveling to the Arctic about 1,200 to 1,600 years ago. Many men disappeared or lost their lives trying to go where no Westerner had been before. In 1610, the Englishman Henry Hudson tried to sail through the waters of the Arctic. But he and his son were killed in a mutiny! The crew took over the ship and set Hudson and his son adrift in a small boat. In 1906, Norwegian explorer Roald Amundsen became the first man to sail across the Arctic Ocean. And after Peary reached the pole in 1909, many other explorers soon followed. Today submarines cross the Arctic under the ice, planes fly over the North Pole, and people travel there using dogsleds and snowmobiles.

From Forest to Ice

If today's travelers had lived 45 million years ago, they would tell us that the Arctic was home to alligators, crocodiles, turtles, snakes, and birds! At that time the Earth was very warm, and the Arctic had swampy forests, like the ones in Florida's Everglades.

But temperatures slowly cooled. Ice began to form at the North and South poles, at either end of the globe. About 15 million years ago, the swampy forests vanished. Two million years ago, in what are known as the *ice ages,* sheets of ice spread across the poles and much of the northern part of the world.

Now the world's climate is somewhere between those long-gone warm days and the ice ages. If you travel to the North Pole today, you won't see any crocodiles or snakes. But you might see polar bears, walruses, seals, reindeer, foxes, owls, and even bumblebees. In the high arctic regions, you would see what Peary described—a polar desert with shifting ice, snow, and water everywhere. But lower in the Arctic you would also see bright blue lakes, shrubs and wildflowers, birds searching for food, squirrels digging in the hard ground, and maybe even a whale resting in a shallow stream.

1

On Top of the World

You may think you know all about the Arctic. It's an icy place where only reindeer and polar bears live, right? Not quite! The Arctic is so cold that your skin could freeze within 30 seconds. All the same, plenty of creatures live there. Seals, foxes, and owls are arctic animals. Animals you may have in your backyard, such as squirrels, hares, and even butterflies, live in the Arctic. The arctic versions of these species have simply *adapted,* or adjusted, to their environment.

The Arctic Circle

Just what is the Arctic Circle? The Arctic Circle itself is actually just a line drawn by mapmakers around the top of the globe at about 66° latitude. Take a look at a globe and find the Arctic Circle. Or if you don't have a globe, think of your Halloween pumpkin. Remember cutting out a circle around the top to make a lid? If your pumpkin were a globe, the line you cut would represent the Arctic Circle. The region above the Arctic Circle, represented by the pumpkin lid, is actually about 15,775,000 square miles. That's about 8 percent of the Earth's surface.

Seven nations fall within the Arctic Circle: Canada, Denmark (which governs the arctic island of Greenland), Finland, Norway (which has some arctic islands), the Soviet Union, Sweden, and the United States (Alaska is the only U.S. state that lies within the arctic region).

Instead of defining the Arctic by this imaginary circle, many scientists use *mean* (average) temperature to define the Arctic. To find the mean temperature of an area, add the hottest and coldest temperatures for the warmest summer month, and divide that figure by two. If that number is less than 50°F, then that place is an arctic region. Fifty degrees may sound warm, but keep in mind that this is for a summer month! During the winter, the temperature goes down to about −30°F.

When it gets that cold, the water that makes up much of the arctic region freezes. In the winter, it's hard to tell if a snow-covered region is land, water, or ice! Arctic waters are covered with two types of ice. *Fast-ice* is ice that forms near or at the edge of land. *Pack-ice* is shifting or moving ice that forms at sea. Surrounding the North Pole is an *ice cap,* an area that is always covered by ice and snow.

Not all arctic regions are slabs of ice, however. In the lower mild regions, called *tundra,* wildflowers bloom, willows line the shores of bright blue lakes, and rivers carry fresh water to the arctic seas. Even in the high arctic zone, which is mainly a polar desert, grass, moss, and *lichens* (very simple brownish plants that live on solid surfaces such as stones or tree trunks) still grow.

Land of the Midnight Sun

How would you like to wake up on a Saturday, spend 3 months playing outdoors, come home when it gets dark, and find that it's still Saturday? In the arctic summer, a day can last for up to 3 months! That's because the sun never sets. The bad news, though, is that there's a long, dark winter as well. For the other 9 months of the year, the sun never rises above the horizon at the North Pole.

Why does this happen? The Earth rotates on an axis through the poles that's slightly off center. This makes the Earth tilt as it rotates. As the Earth *orbits,* or travels, around the sun, the tilt causes first the North Pole, then the South Pole to turn toward the sun. This gives us the four seasons.

In the wintertime, the North Pole is tilting

as far away from the sun as possible. So if you were standing at the North Pole, you would get only slanting rays from the sun because it is so low in the sky. For 9 months, the sun never really rises. During the summer, the opposite is true. When the North Pole tilts toward the sun, the sun's rays shine on the Arctic 24 hours a day.

Tricks of the Trade

All the creatures that live in the Arctic have special strategies, or tricks, to help them survive the cold climate. Some fish and insects even have "antifreeze" in their blood to prevent it from freezing during the winter! Of course, the best way to survive the long winter is to move south. Many animals, especially birds, do just that. But the really tough arctic animals use other strategies. Some small land animals, such as squirrels, go into a deep sleep called *hibernation*. During this time their body temperatures drop and their hearts beat very, very slowly. It takes days to go into as well as out of this state of hibernation.

For some animals, another good strategy is simply being built for the cold. Anything that allows the animals to keep body heat in, and the cold winds out, helps them to survive. In the same way that people put on down coats and snow boots, an arctic fox grows a thick white coat of fur for the winter. Like the polar bear's, its paws are covered, top and bottom, with this fur.

It may not surprise you to learn that foxes and bears have furry pads to keep their feet warm, but did you know that birds do, too? Both owls and ravens have special foot pads that keep the heat in and the cold out. These birds adopt the same strategy as land animals and put on a thick winter coat. The *ptarmigan*, for example, is a bird that grows more feathers for the cold winter.

Imagine wearing a woolly undershirt all winter. It sounds itchy and horrible, doesn't it? But the musk-ox has one. It also has an overcoat made of thick, shaggy brown hair that almost reaches the ground. You would definitely want a coat like this for those arctic lows of −90°F!

Some small animals can't *insulate,* or protect, themselves from the cold that well. For this reason, instead of making their own insulation, they look for it in the environment. But in the Arctic, what else is there but snow? Many small animals and birds make burrows or nests in the snow and spend the winter in these warm white homes.

Just as desert plants and animals have tricks that enable them to survive, so, too, do all arctic animals have strategies that keep them going during the long winters. Do you think *you* could adapt?

2

King of the North

A shaggy white beast slowly makes its way across the frozen north, moving from ice to water and back. It stops to investigate a new smell or strange plant, or to touch noses with a friend. At the water's edge, it takes a swipe at a seal with one of its huge white paws and kills it. A helicopter buzzes overhead. The great white bear sits back on its haunches and takes a swipe at that, too, as if to say, "Come any closer and I'll knock you out of the sky!" This is the *polar bear,* the Arctic's magnificent king.

The Big White Bear

The polar bear has earned its nicknames— Lord of the Arctic and King of the North. Scientists think it *evolved,* or developed, from a type of brown bear that existed about 50,000 to 100,000 years ago. Today polar bears live in all parts of the Arctic, but most live in Canada. The bears seem to live in groups. Like many arctic animals, the polar bear was once threatened by hunters, but the majestic animal is now protected by law. Scientists estimate that there are about 25,000 polar bears.

The polar bear is the largest omnivore living on land in the Arctic. An *omnivore* is an animal that eats meat as well as fruits and plants. Twice the size of a lion or tiger, the average adult male polar bear is about 5 feet high at the shoulder. The largest one ever seen was more than 11 feet tall! It can weigh up to 900 pounds.

Female polar bears are shorter than the males but weigh about the same. The large size of the polar bear doesn't slow it down, though. It can run, swim, and leap better than any Olympic gold medalist. Do you know of any human being who can run 35 miles per hour, swim 6 miles per hour, and leap 15 feet?

The polar bear has a long body, slender legs, and paws that are designed for life in the Arctic. The larger an animal's paw, the easier it is to walk in snow. A polar bear's paws are almost 1 foot across. The wide paws act like snowshoes, spreading the bear's weight over a bigger area to keep it from sinking in the snow. Its toes are partially webbed, making the polar bear a very powerful swimmer.

The polar bear's paws are also covered with fur, which helps it to grip the slippery ice.

The polar bear actually lives on the floating pack-ice, moving along with its flow. Having fur-covered paws gives the bear another advantage. When you walk on ice, the sound is magnified. If you're hunting, you need to be as quiet as possible. With fur-coated paws, the polar bear can silently sneak up on its *prey* (the animals it hunts for food).

Keeping Warm

The polar bear's furry paws are only one of the many ways in which the animal has adapted to its frozen environment. It also has a thick fur coat to keep it warm. The polar bear has two layers of fur, a ground layer of short hair and a guard layer of longer hair. This guard hair is hollow, which helps the polar bear to float in water. The hair also contains an oil that repels water, making it run right off the bear before it can get close to its skin. Underneath this fur coat, the polar bear has a layer of fat that can be as many as 4 inches thick. The bear can survive even when the temperature drops to −70°F because this fat keeps its body heat trapped inside.

In addition to coping with the cold, arctic animals have to protect themselves against the glare of the sun. The summer sun reflecting off the shiny white ice and snow would give anyone a headache! In fact, mountaineers often suffer from *snow blindness,* which they say feels as if someone had thrown sand into their eyes. It comes from having the surface of the pupils burned by the glare from the ice and snow. But this doesn't happen to the polar bear because it has a type of third eyelid to protect it. This *membrane* is a thin, flexible sheet of internal tissue. The polar bear has no eyelashes because they would freeze in the cold.

Sleeping in Snow

A polar bear sometimes walks 25 miles in one day in search of food. If it has to, it can walk steadily for 24 hours and cover about 50 miles. Polar bears are most active during the summer. But even during the winter, the male bear walks the ice and hunts when it is not hibernating. It has to rely on smell and whatever light is reflected off the snow to guide it. When there's a very strong blizzard, the animal digs a shelter in the snow.

The polar bears that live far north, high in the Arctic, don't try to survive outside during the brutal winter. In October, they build dens in the dense snowbanks that form on the sides of hills and valleys. They then go into the dens for a long nap. While they're sleeping, their heartbeats slow down. Their body temperatures drop a little, too. In addition, the bears don't eat at all and must live off the fat they have stored in their bodies during the summer. Polar bears are not true hibernators, however. When an animal hibernates, all its body functions slow down, its body temperature drops drastically, and it sleeps very soundly. Unlike a true hibernator, a polar bear can wake up within a second.

Bringing Up Baby

In the far north, both male and female polar bears build dens because they want to escape the long, cold winter. But in the warmer parts of the Arctic, usually only the female spends the winter in a den—and not to avoid the cold, but to have babies.

Polar bears usually mate in May. By October, the females are ready to move into their dens. As winter sets in and snow begins to cover the entrance, the females make holes in the roof of the den so they can breathe.

In December, each female polar bear gives birth to one or two cubs. The cubs are so small that they could fit in your hand! Weighing only about 1½ pounds, they don't open their eyes until they are more than a month old. The cubs remain in the den for a few months in order to keep warm; gain strength and nourishment from their mother's rich, fatty milk; and stay well out of sight of *predators,* or enemies. Some dens have two sections: a main area for the mother to sleep in and a playroom for the cubs to play in!

By the end of March, the mother is ready to come out of the den. With a few smacks of her strong paws, the entrance to the den is opened again and the new cubs emerge for the first time. At this point they weigh between 20 and 25 pounds. Cubs stay with their mothers during their first year and even share a den the next winter. By the beginning of their second year, however, they are ready to learn how to hunt and fend for themselves.

Seal Hunt

If it had a choice, the polar bear would have an all-seal diet. It spends long hours walking along the pack-ice, searching the water for signs of seals. Polar bears have an excellent sense of smell to help them in their hunt.

A polar bear sometimes stalks its prey on land, flattening itself to the ground. The polar bear will even cover its black nose with its paw so that it is entirely *camouflaged,* or hidden, by the snow. A polar bear can also slip into the water and float along, pretending it is a piece of ice. When it gets close to a sun-bathing seal, it springs out of the water and kills the seal with one blow.

Some seals make dens below the surface of the snow. If the polar bear manages to sniff out the den, which it often does, it scrapes away the outer layer of frozen ice. It then stands on its hind legs and falls onto the snow, all 900 pounds of its huge body crashing through the den. When the roof of the den collapses, the seal and its pups are exposed and become easy prey for the polar bear.

If there are many seals around, a polar bear eats one seal every few days. It eats the seal with great care, feasting only on the *blubber* (the fat just underneath the skin) and the *entrails* (the inner parts of the seal's body). Eating blubber may seem horrible to you, but it's very good for the polar bear. It has lots of nutrients and is very fattening. A polar bear can eat 150 pounds of blubber during a single meal. If the bear is very hungry, it will eat more of the seal. But it usually leaves the rest behind. One animal, the arctic fox, is well aware of the polar bear's eating habits and takes advantage of them. The fox is often seen trailing behind the polar bear, waiting for it to kill a seal, eat the blubber, and leave the rest, which the fox then eats.

The polar bear also eats fruits and plants— and just about anything else. If there are no seals around, the bear eats eggs from birds' nests, ducks, grass, seaweed, crowberries, and cranberries. Polar bears are scavengers, too. If they live near humans, they will go through camps, tents, and garbage cans in their search for food.

In fact, there is one town that is famous for its scavenging polar bears. The town of Churchill, on the western shore of Canada's Hudson Bay, has so many polar bears that it is called the polar bear capital of the world. When the sea ice melts during the summer, the seals swim to colder areas and the bears are left without food. They wander the coast eating whatever they can find. The town garbage dump is a favorite picnic spot for the hungry bears. Tourists now flock to Churchill by the thousands, where they are guaranteed to see polar bears—though a polar bear nosing through human garbage is not quite a polar bear in its *habitat,* or natural home.

Bear Behavior

Polar bears are very curious animals and they are not easily frightened. When they see something new, they usually stop to investigate. One reason they are so fearless is that they have few natural enemies. Only a killer whale or a pack of hungry, desperate wolves would dare to attack a polar bear.

Polar bears are also very playful and enjoy romping in the snow. Cubs play with one another, running and tumbling head over heels. When two adults meet, they walk around each other in smaller and smaller circles and finally touch noses. Then, standing on their back legs, they fight playfully, pushing and boxing and making grunting sounds.

The crew of a Canadian Coast Guard ship tells an interesting story about a polar bear they met. They came upon a polar bear and threw it a steak. Not surprisingly, the bear climbed aboard the ship! Since this wasn't quite what the crew wanted, they decided to scare the bear off by spraying it with a hose. But this didn't frighten the polar bear—it loved the water!

White Magic

The powerful polar bear has awed humans for centuries—and taught us a few lessons as well. It's thought that the Inuit Eskimos learned how to hunt seals by copying the behavior of the polar bear or by following polar bears to seal dens. The Inuit both respect and fear the great white bear. For some, the polar bear is a god who has wisdom and magic powers. They believe that humans can absorb these magical powers by wearing a necklace with a polar bear's tooth on it. The Inuit also think that the polar bear has a spirit which leaves its body when it dies.

Bear Survival

The polar bear has only one true enemy: humans. Polar bears have been hunted for their skins and meat for thousands of years. Although the Inuit worship the polar bear, they also need the animal in order to survive. They have traditionally hunted the polar bear, prizing its meat and skin. They wear bear mittens, boots, and trousers, and sleep on bear rugs. Bearskins are used to cover shields and boats, and grease from bear fur oils their sled runners. Foreign hunters used to trade polar bear skins and furs.

For many years scientists and conservationists have been working in the Arctic, researching and trying to protect the polar bear. In 1965, all the arctic nations agreed to protect the polar bear. It became illegal to kill any female polar bear with a cub. Then, in 1973, in the first formal agreement ever made on an arctic issue, these nations passed the International Agreement on the Conservation of Polar Bears and Their Habitats. In 1981, they voted to make the agreement a permanent one.

According to this agreement, the polar bear is now protected from hunters, though the Inuit are allowed to kill some bears for their survival. The polar bear remains threatened, however, by industrial development of the Arctic. Companies searching for oil use up valuable space. Oil spills endanger seals, and without seals, the polar bears will go hungry. Animals that are sick and malnourished can't survive in the harsh Arctic. It's important that we protect the polar bear before it's too late.

3

Land Lovers: The Arctic's Large Land Mammals

There are more than 4,000 *species,* or kinds, of land mammals in the world. *Mammals* are warm-blooded animals that give birth to live babies (as opposed to eggs) and produce milk to feed them. Of these 4,000, only 48 species live in the Arctic. Arctic mammals include rodents, hares, foxes, wolves, bears, and deer.

Santa's Helpers

We might never have heard of reindeer if it weren't for popular Santa Claus myths in which Santa's sleigh is pulled by a team of flying reindeer. But these stories grew out of actual facts. Reindeer have been tamed and used to draw sleds for thousands of years.

Reindeer are members of the deer family. In fact, three members of the deer family live in the Arctic: the caribou, the moose, and the musk-ox. Caribou and reindeer are two names for the same animal. What we call a *caribou* in North America is called a reindeer in Europe and Asia. The *moose* is the largest member of the deer family. The *musk-ox* lives only in the Arctic and looks like a shaggy brown buffalo with large curved horns.

Caribou appeared in North America sometime during the past 1 million years. Scientists think they came to Asia and Europe by crossing the Bering Strait. This is a 40-mile-wide channel of water between Alaska and the Soviet Union, two landmasses that were once connected by a bridge of land and ice.

For centuries people in Lapland, a northern Scandinavian region, have tamed reindeer and put them to work drawing sleds. The Lapps herd reindeer the way other people herd cattle. They also drink the reindeer's milk, eat its meat, and use its skin.

Hair and Hooves

A caribou is about the same size as a donkey, but it's much heavier than it looks. A grown male, about 4 feet high at the shoulder, can weigh up to 550 pounds. Caribou look like ordinary deer, but they're bigger and huskier. Also, when you see a herd of ordinary deer, you can tell the males from the females because the females don't have antlers. Caribou are an exception to this rule, however, because the females have antlers, too!

Caribou antlers form two heavy main branches. Males shed their antlers in November, during the cold winter months, and grow new ones during the spring. Females keep their antlers through the winter and shed them after giving birth to calves during the summer.

Like polar bears, caribou also have a few strategies that help them survive in the cold arctic climate. Their thick fur is an inch long, and their dense, woolly undercoat covers everything—even their noses and ears. During the winter, their coat changes color, going from a dull brown to a snowy white. This keeps the caribou camouflaged so that their enemies, the wolves, can't see them as well.

Caribou fur is very thick because each hair is hollow. Their coats serve as life jackets that help them float. Caribou are excellent swimmers. They're not very fast, but they can cover long distances as they search for new hunting grounds.

Caribou have a special way of finding food in the middle of the winter when the land is barren and icy. Each of their hooves is wide and splayed, with a very sharp edge. During the winter, the elastic, horny surface in the middle of the sole gets absorbed. This makes the hoof *concave* (hollowed out), leaving the edges exposed—like an overturned glass with a sharp rim. This allows the caribou to scrape through all but the thickest ice in their search for food.

Caribou eat lichens, plants that look like rust-colored moss. In fact, lichens are sometimes called reindeer moss because they are the chief food of the caribou, or reindeer.

Major Migrations

Caribou have a very difficult life. They must avoid being hunted by wolves and humans, and they have to scrape for food during the icy winters. One of the biggest threats to caribou is that wolves prey on their newborn baby calves. Caribou mothers almost always produce healthy calves, but as many as half of them may die during their first few months. They are usually killed by wolves.

To avoid the slaughter of their babies, caribou migrate across long distances, farther than any other deer. During the spring, massive herds of caribou start their journey north. They pass through places where plants are just beginning to grow or bud. Here they graze heavily, stuffing themselves with all kinds of grasses, berries, and mushrooms.

The caribou search for summer homes that are rocky and barren. Calves are born in May and June, often near arctic waters. Then the herds move from the coasts to the foothills of the mountains to escape the mosquitoes in the low-lying swamp-like areas. By September, the snow begins to fall and the caribou move south again for the winter. Reindeer in the Soviet Arctic make a 600-mile-long trek twice a year!

The Biggest Deer

Everything about the moose is big. It has big antlers, big shoulders, a big nose, and big feet. A grown male can be 6 feet tall at the shoulder and weigh more than 1,200 pounds! The average 6-foot-tall human weighs only about 160 to 170 pounds. The American moose is also sometimes called an *elk*.

You can spot a moose by its grayish brown coat, long legs, long and fleshy nose, and its spectacular antlers. Unlike the caribou, only male moose have antlers. Moose antlers can spread as wide as 6 feet!

Moose live mainly in the Canadian and Alaskan regions of the Arctic. Like all arctic animals, moose behavior depends on the season. During the summer, moose live in small groups. Calves are born in May and June. Moose, like reindeer, are bothered by flies and mosquitoes. Many groups travel from the warm tundra region to the coast of the Arctic Ocean in order to escape the annoying pests.

In September and October, the mating season begins. The males get restless and tend to pick fights. The breeding season is called a *rut*. The velvet-like fur that lines the males' antlers falls off and they *spar,* or fight, one another, locking antlers. No one is sure why they do this. Males mate with several females. They call them with a loud bellow.

Moose migrate to warmer regions during the winter. The moose is long-legged and clumsy, especially in the deep winter snow. This makes them easy prey for wolves. Moose use their hooves and antlers to protect themselves from their enemies.

Outfoxing the Others

Of all the arctic creatures, the fox is probably the one that is best equipped to survive. It can live in the coldest temperatures and find food almost anywhere. For one thing, the *arctic fox* isn't a choosy eater. It eats almost any animal! It's an omnivore that preys on hares, musk-oxen, seabirds, ducks and geese, seal pups, fish, and insects.

The arctic fox's favorite food, however, is the lemming. A *lemming* is a small, short-tailed brown animal that looks like a cross between a squirrel and a guinea pig. When lemming populations are high, fox populations are high in that area, and 90 percent of the fox's diet is made up of lemmings. When lemmings are scarce, the fox moves to coastal regions and hunts for fish and seabirds. The fox can also be seen following polar bears to eat parts of seals that are left behind. If food really becomes scarce, the fox even follows the polar bear out onto the pack-ice—and hopes for leftovers!

The fox has a big impact on the population of other animals. When there are lots of foxes, look out! One fox in northwest Alaska is reported to have crossed a mud flat at low tide, then swum to a nearby island where a colony of a type of duck called an *eider* was nesting. The fox killed at least one female eider and took about 500 eggs!

The arctic fox's other special feature is its ability to survive extreme temperatures. It doesn't need to hibernate and can stay active all year long. It makes dens by burrowing into the soil. Some of these dens have only one entrance, but others have as many as eighty! During the spring and summer, arctic foxes raise their young in these dens.

During the winter, the arctic fox grows a thick coat that keeps it well insulated. It changes color from gray or reddish brown to white. Fur covers the top and bottom of its paws. About the size of a large cat, the fox is so well insulated that it doesn't need to produce more heat until the air temperature drops to −40°F. Even then, the fox requires only a small increase in its *metabolism* (the ability to turn food into energy) to survive. An arctic fox could sleep for an hour in the open snow with no loss in body temperature even if the thermometer dropped to −112°F.

4

More Than Just a Rodent

The larger arctic mammals, such as the reindeer, polar bear, and fox, are the popular ones. Their pictures can always be seen on posters and in magazines. But the small mammals deserve some attention, too. The rodents are among the most interesting small mammals in the Arctic.

You might think all rodents are unpleasant, rat-like creatures that are just one step above insects. But beavers, squirrels, voles, marmots, and lemmings are rodents, too. A rodent can be identified by its teeth—it has strong incisor, or cutting, teeth but no sharp, pointy canine teeth. In fact, the word *rodent* comes from the Latin word *rodere*, which means "to gnaw."

Legendary Cliff Divers

When people think of lemmings, they imagine hundreds of small, brown short-tailed animals lining up to jump off a cliff as if they were committing mass suicide. These are *Norwegian lemmings.* They do not live in the Arctic. But their close relatives, the *arctic* and *brown lemmings,* do.

The Norwegian lemming doesn't kill itself on purpose. What happens is that the population rises and falls in cycles, going from very high to very low and back. When the number of lemmings becomes so high that not all of them can exist in the same place, they *migrate,* or move from one region to another, spreading in all directions in a frenzy. Some rush inland, while others are forced toward the coast. When they reach the coast, they jump into the water and swim, hoping to reach land. They actually swim until they become exhausted and finally drown. They are not sacrificing themselves, just searching for a new place in which to live. Unfortunately, many of them never find one.

Arctic and brown lemmings don't behave in this manner, but they, too, have population swings that go from one extreme to the other.

No one is quite sure why lemming populations have such marked cycles. On an average of every 4 years, the population drops significantly. Then it slowly rebuilds to a peak only to fall again. The crashes occur during the summer months, when birds of prey, weasels, foxes, wolves, and polar bears hunt the lemming.

In order for the lemming population to increase, the animals need three things. First, they need to have few predators to have to protect themselves from. Second, they need to have lots of food available. Lemmings are *herbivores,* which means they eat no meat, only grass, shrubs, leaves, and other plants. Third, they need a good snowpack so they can make nests for their babies. Underneath a deep and steady cover of snow, female lemmings build elaborate nests out of plants. The snow insulates the nest, keeping the lemmings nice and warm.

During the winter, lemmings turn white for better camouflage, and their claws become larger to help them forage for food. They adapt to the cold very well and do many other things that help them to survive. But unlike other small mammals, they graze in fields during the winter and eat absolutely all the food that is available. This is bad for the field in the long run and could even decrease the amount of food that is available to them in years to come. How this animal lives is a constant source of wonder and study for scientists.

Sleeping It Off

What would you do during winter if the temperature dropped well below freezing, there were no sunlight for months, and there weren't much food available? How about taking a very long nap? That's what two arctic rodents, the *arctic ground squirrel* and the *Alaskan marmot,* do. True hibernators, they go into a deep sleep from late September or early October until March or April.

You would have no trouble recognizing the arctic ground squirrel because it looks very much like other North American squirrels. The Alaskan marmot is a cousin of the North American prairie marmot—also called a prairie dog because its cry sounds like a bark. It is stout, has short legs, and looks a little like a weasel.

These rodents store up a lot of fat in their bodies to prepare for hibernation. They build dens or burrows and line them with leaves, lichens, and musk-ox hair. During the fall, over a period of a few days, their body temperature drops to below freezing or whatever the air temperature is. Their heartbeats go from 80 times per minute to just 5 times per minute! They lose consciousness completely, unlike hibernating polar bears, and it takes them a few days to wake up when spring comes.

Squirreling Away

The arctic ground squirrel lives off stored fat while it hibernates. As you can imagine, they need to eat a lot just before hibernating.

Adult squirrels can store 350 grams of fat in the 60 or 70 days before they go into hibernation. This increases their body fat by almost 20 percent. They save energy by sleeping at night. This might not sound so unusual, but don't forget that during an arctic summer there is daylight all the time. The squirrels go into their dens and sleep even though it is light out.

Some squirrels and other rodents build very complex systems of *burrows,* large underground tunnels, that are more confusing than any maze. Other animals invade these burrows to keep warm during winter, whether the squirrels invite them or not!

Unfortunately, although the squirrel's cycle of fattening and hibernating is crucial to its survival, not all of them can do it. Some do not store enough fat, and others are too frail to prepare properly. This is especially true of young squirrels. Of all the newly born females that are born in the spring, half do not make it through the winter. And only one out of ten of all the newly born males manages to reach its first birthday.

Only a killer whale or a pack of wolves would dare attack
a polar bear.

This polar bear isn't having any trouble leaping from one icy ledge to another—even though it weighs about 900 pounds!

A polar bear stretches after a long winter nap.

Polar bear cubs stay with their mother until they are about 2 years old.

The moose is the largest member of the deer family. Only the male moose has antlers, which spread as wide as 6 feet!

The gyrfalcon lives in the Arctic year-round. Most of its diet consists of the ptarmigan, another arctic bird of prey.

You can tell this is a ringed seal pup by the small, pale rings or spots that cover its dark gray body.

This harp seal rests on the pack-ice in the Gulf of St. Lawrence.

A walrus uses its tusks to dig for food along the ocean floor. Its coarse whiskers act as feelers to guide it through murky water.

Every year hundreds of walruses flop onto the beaches of Round Island in Alaska to shed their skins.

The 12-foot-long beluga is the most common arctic whale. It is known as the "sea canary" because of the many sounds it makes.

The innocent-looking arctic fox will prey on almost anything when food is scarce.

The claws of the lemming become larger during the winter to help it forage for food in snow-covered fields.

The Norwegian reindeer turns from brown to white in
the winter for protection against predators.

5

In Cold Water: Arctic Marine Mammals

Even though the water is ice-cold and there are chunks of ice floating everywhere, many fish and marine mammals live in arctic waters. Walruses and certain species of seals and whales have all adapted to the cold and the ice. These marine mammals have something else in common: They have all been or are still being hunted by humans.

Tough Tusks

There's no mistaking a *walrus.* The powerful, slick brown creatures are usually seen lying heavily on a pack of ice, displaying their long white tusks. Their coarse white whiskers and droopy skin give them a sad but curious look. When early European explorers saw these huge beasts, they called them sea horses.

Walruses weigh a ton—really! The average adult male weighs between 2,600 and 3,500 pounds, or about 1½ tons, even though it's only about 10 feet long.

One unique arctic sight is the annual walrus *molt,* when the walruses shed their outer skin. To do this, hundreds of them come out of the water and flop onto small arctic islands. Groups of walruses lie in the sun, sharing whatever warmth there is and huddling together for protection from predators.

The walrus's tusk is its most outstanding feature. Both male and female walruses have tusks that continue to grow throughout their lives. The tusks are really canine teeth that grow from the animal's upper jaw. Atlantic walruses have tusks that are about 1 foot long, while the tusks of Pacific walruses can grow 3 feet long and weigh up to 11 pounds. Imagine having a tooth that's as long as your arm!

Why did the walrus develop such big tusks? Scientists have a few theories. One is that walruses grew larger and larger canine teeth to help them dig for food along the ocean floor. A walrus will take a dive—anywhere from 2 to 8 minutes long—to depths of 240 feet and drag its tusks along the ocean bottom to gather food. The long, coarse white whiskers also help, acting as feelers to guide the animals through murky water. To get enough food, a walrus searches nearly 50 square yards of seabed every day! Any food that it roots out, such as an arctic clam, gets sucked up. The walrus uses its big, heavy lips and tongue to separate seafood from its shell. It has a small mouth and can create a lot of suction to get its food.

Another theory about the walrus's tusk is that it is used in much the same way a mountain climber uses an ice pick. Walruses can live either on pack-ice or fast-ice. In order to be able to haul their 1-ton bodies out of the water and onto the ice, they stick their tusks into the ice and grab hold. They may also use their tusks to make breathing holes in the ice.

A third theory is that a walrus's tusk has something to do with its social status, or position. The bigger the tusk, the higher the walrus's rank in the group.

Walruses are attacked by killer whales and occasionally polar bears. But humans are their main threat. During the 1700's and 1800's, walruses were hunted along with whales for their oil and their ivory tusks. Walruses are not protected by international law. They are still hunted in Soviet and Alaskan waters, but hunting is now strictly regulated in Canada. However, the demand for walrus meat in Canada has dropped. Why? Walrus meat is used to make dog food, but dog teams are no longer being used as the main form of transportation across the Canadian Arctic. Fewer dog teams means less need for dog food, so fewer walruses are killed.

Seal Family Trees

Seals fall mainly into two very different families. One family, called *Otaridae,* has fur and ears and can move easily when out of water. These seals visit the Arctic, but they usually *breed* (have their babies) on land and spend most of their time in warmer waters.

The other seal family, called *Phocidae,* has no ears, has short flippers, and has difficulty moving out of water. Sometimes called *hair seals,* these are the seals that live in the Arctic. They may be called hair seals, but they don't really have hair. They don't have fur either. They rely on a thick layer of fat, or blubber, to keep themselves warm.

Their short flippers help them to survive in cold water. You know how your toes and fingers are the first things that get cold during the winter? That's because a lot of heat escapes through these *appendages,* or smaller limbs of the body. The fewer appendages you have, or the smaller they are, the warmer you'll be because less heat escapes.

These seals can also breed either on land or at sea. They live on pack-ice, and the amount of ice available each year is the key to their survival. Most seals give birth to their young on pack-ice. If there is very little pack-ice, or there are no good places on the pack-ice for giving birth, the seals are in trouble. They may be unable to give birth safely.

The Ringed Seal

The *ringed seal* looks like a seal with freckles. Small pale rings or spots cover its dark grayish body, and its sides and belly are a silver-gray color. These are the seals that are best adapted to the arctic climate. For one thing, the ringed seal is the only seal that can survive in areas of fast-ice. Other kinds of seals live on pack-ice, out in the middle of the water.

Most seals come out of the water and give birth to their pups on pack-ice. But not the ringed seals. The female seals dig out small lairs just under the surface of the snow on land. They use the claws on their front flippers to dig out the lairs, which are then connected to the ocean by a breathing hole through the ice. They keep the holes open by scratching constantly. The females give birth in these lairs, which keep their newborn pups warm as well as safe from foxes and polar bears that might want a seal-pup supper. These lairs can't be made everywhere, however. Only certain spots are just right for them. Good ice conditions are therefore very important to the survival of the ringed seal.

Fake Beards and False Noses

The *bearded seal* has dense, drooping, coarse whiskers that look like a thin, scraggly beard. These act as a sixth sense for the seal. Like the walrus, the bearded seal uses its whiskers to find food. It sometimes copies the ringed seal and makes breathing holes and lairs below the snow. Usually, however, the bearded seal gives birth to its pups on pack-ice.

Bearded seals live throughout the Arctic. They and the *harp seals,* whose babies have beautiful snow-white fur for the first few weeks of their lives, have been heavily hunted by the Inuit Eskimos in Canada, Alaska, and Greenland. The seals are hunted both for food and leather to line boots and cover boats. (Greenpeace and other groups are working hard to protect seals and other marine mammals from hunters.)

Another Arctic seal is the *hooded seal,* which lives in the northwest Atlantic. This seal gets its name from the large cavity in its nasal passages. When it feels threatened by intruders, the hooded seal can *inflate,* or blow up, this cavity to form a crest on the top of its nose. It can even inflate a part of its inner nose out through its left nostril to form what looks like a red balloon!

Whales Ahoy!

If the water you lived in were filled with bits of floating ice, you can imagine that having a fin sticking out of your back just might get in the way. That's why the three kinds of whales that live in the Arctic don't have a *dorsal,* or back, fin. Many whales, such as the orca, or killer whale, and the huge blue whale, cruise in and out of the arctic waters. Only the bowhead whale, beluga whale, and narwhal have dropped the dorsal fin in order to be year-round residents of the Arctic.

The *bowhead* whale is known to be a master ice-cracker. Its head comes to a peak just where its twin blowholes are. This peak helps it break up ice. In fact, it has been known to break through pieces of ice that are almost 2 feet thick!

The bowhead gets its name from its jaw, which is shaped like an upside-down bow. Bowheads have *baleen* instead of teeth. Long, thin blades, or plates, of baleen grow down from each side of the whale's upper jaw. They are made of keratin, the same material that's found in your fingernails. A bowhead eats by swimming with its mouth open and trapping shrimp-like creatures called *krill* in these triangular baleen plates. It dislodges the krill from the baleen plates with its enormous tongue and then swallows them.

Bowhead whales are part of a group called *right* whales. They got their name because hunters thought they were the "right" whales to kill: They are big (up to 60 feet long), they are slow swimmers, and they float when they are dead (this made them easy to tow behind a whaling boat). All right whales, especially the bowhead, were hunted so much during the last century that they almost became *extinct,* or gone forever.

The *beluga* whale, also called the white whale, is the most common arctic whale. A small whale, it's only about 12 or 14 feet long. The beluga lives in open water during the winter, then travels to the northernmost Arctic for the summer. There it seeks out shallow rivers, where it lies for a few weeks with its belly touching the sand or gravel and its back way out of the water. Like the walrus, the beluga, too, has an annual molt during which it rubs and scratches itself to help shed the outer layer of its skin. These rivers are fully booked up for July and August, when parties of belugas each spend a few weeks there!

The beluga has been nicknamed the sea canary because of its remarkable ability to make all kinds of unusual sounds—toots, trills, whistles, squawks, croaks, and growls. Scientists are not quite sure what all these sounds mean. Some of them seem to be the belugas' way of "talking" to one another. Other noises may help the whales figure out exactly where they are, and in what direction they are traveling.

The *narwhal* is the unicorn of the seas. It is the only whale that has a tusk. The tusk is really a canine tooth, growing through the upper left lip, that can grow up to 11 feet long. The whales themselves are usually about 16 feet long. The tusk is twisted like a spiral, making it look a little like a unicorn's horn. Scientists are not sure just what the tusk is for. Only male narwhals grow tusks, and they use them to dominate other males. Some scientists believe that the narwhal may also use the tusk to defend itself against polar bears.

The narwhal faces many threats to its survival. Both killer whales and polar bears are its enemies, and it also can become trapped in ice. Humans have hunted the narwhal as well, especially for its ivory tusk—so much so that these creatures can now be seen only in the high arctic waters of Canada. If this continues, the unicorn of the sea will sadly become only a memory, an imaginary creature for future generations.

6

Winging It: Birds and Insects in the Arctic

Fighting, losing limbs, living in another animal's nose, freezing solid for 4 months, flying thousands of miles—birds and insects do all these things in order to survive in the Arctic. Almost 200 species of birds live or breed in the Arctic, along with about 2,000 species of spiders, flies, bees, ants, wasps, beetles, and butterflies. There are no snakes or frogs in the Arctic. These cold-blooded animals could not survive in or adapt to the cold. Unlike warm-blooded animals, cold-blooded animals can't change the temperature of their blood. This means that their blood temperature is usually the same as the temperature of the air around them. A snake's blood would freeze in the Arctic.

For the Birds!

Most arctic birds go to the Arctic only to

48

breed and spend the summer. During the 3 summer months, it is always daytime. Flowers and small shrubs bloom, and birds can find plenty of food in the wet, boggy tundra. But few birds like the 9 long months of winter there. Most of them migrate south, sometimes flying thousands of miles to find a better home. The arctic *tern* likes the icy conditions of the Arctic, but hates the cold, so during the winter it flies about 10,875 miles to the Antarctic because summer is just beginning there.

Of all the species of birds that breed or live in the Arctic, only about six or eight actually stay there year-round. Of these year-round residents, the ptarmigan and the *redpoll* have adapted to the cold like the mammals have.

When winter comes, the ptarmigan grows more feathers, even on its nose, and lowers its metabolism so that it can spend its energy wisely. Its feathers turn from brown to white, to give it greater camouflage in the snow. In the same way that small mammals burrow into the snow, ptarmigans and redpolls may spend the night buried under the snow, *conserving,* or saving, all their body heat. They also have heavy feathers or fringed scales on their feet called snowshoe feathers. This allows them to walk on the snow or frozen ground without getting too cold.

A Wise Move

The ptarmigan is pretty good at conserving the heat its body makes, but it could learn a few things from the snowy owl. This year-round arctic resident is a survival expert. It loses three or four times less body heat than the ptarmigan does. Not only does the snowy owl have heavily feathered legs and feet, it also has hardened bumps on the bottom of its feet so only small parts of its foot pads actually need to touch the cold ground. These bumps are so well designed that very little heat passes through them. One of the lowest temperatures ever recorded in the Northern Hemisphere was −80.5°F. Who was one of the survivors? The snowy owl.

The snowy owl has white feathers all year, though the female can be flecked with gray or black feathers. Its heavy-lidded eyes and narrow beak give it a contented look.

The snowy owl's favorite food is the lemming. Since the lemming's population changes, going from large to small and back, so does the owl's. The owl even uses lemming bodies to line its nest. An adult owl eats anywhere from 600 to 1,600 lemmings a year.

Another year-round arctic bird is the *gyrfalcon*, a large falcon that lives throughout the arctic region. This is bad luck for the ptarmigan because the gyrfalcon is a skilled bird of prey. The ptarmigan makes up 95 per-

cent of the gyrfalcon's diet. It also preys on
snow buntings (small birds related to the
finch), seabirds, lemmings, and hares.

No Penguins Here

You may be wondering about penguins.
These seabirds live on ice and snow—but not
in the Arctic. Penguins live only in the Southern Hemisphere, or southern half of the
globe. Seven types of penguins live in the
Antarctic, near the South Pole. Penguins are
used to life on the thick, solid ice of Antarc-
tica. Who knows whether they would be able
to survive on the moving ice of the Arctic?

Small, Dark, and Hairy

There's a rule among animals in the Arctic:
the farther north, the whiter the animals.
White animals are able to camouflage themselves in the snow. But insects don't follow
this rule. The farther north they go, the
smaller, darker, and hairier they become.

This happens for good reason, too. Have
you ever worn a black shirt on a hot, sunny
day? You may have gotten so hot that you had
to go home and change into a lighter-colored
shirt. Black absorbs heat, while white reflects
it. This means that a small black spider keeps
in all the heat it can absorb from the sun.

Hair also helps to absorb the sun's heat and keeps the body well insulated.

Arctic insects are devoted sunbathers. Butterflies, moths, and flies sun themselves as much as possible, tilting their wings to get the maximum sun. Flies even sunbathe inside flowers, where the heat from the sun gathers and makes a hot little room! They need all the heat they can get.

Of all the arctic insects, only the bumblebee can make its own heat. It does this by beating its wings back and forth rapidly. Think how hard this small bumblebee has to work! On an average, the air is −30°F during the winter and may be only as warm as 50°F during the summer. If a thermometer were placed in the bee's nest as the insect heated it to raise its young, the reading would be 86°F!

Arctic insects also use some of the same strategies that mammals use. Remember how seals have smaller appendages that allow them to conserve body heat? In the same way, Arctic insects have smaller legs or wings than their non-arctic cousins do. Some flies or moths even get rid of their wings completely. In some species, the females simply don't grow wings. Why don't they need wings? One theory is that being wingless allows the moths to conserve valuable body heat. Another theory is that they will be more stable during windy conditions!

Chilling Out

Arctic insects have one major problem during the winter. How can they keep their tiny bodies from freezing? Some use a cooling system that keeps them warm even when the temperature is below freezing. Their bodies produce *glycerol,* a syrupy liquid of sugar and protein that comes from fat and prevents ice crystals from forming in their bodies.

Not all insects can do this, however. Many adult insects aren't equipped to make it through the winter. Instead, their eggs and *larvae* (the form an insect takes after it hatches from an egg and before it becomes an adult) survive because they are able to withstand freezing or just above freezing temperatures. Some adults can *dehydrate,* or get rid of all the liquid in their bodies, so they won't freeze. Others have systems that limit the freezing to only one part of their body. As you can imagine, most adults are not active during the winter.

The queen bee is the only bee that can live through the cold, arctic winter. She emerges in spring and finds a good place to nest. Often she uses a burrow that was built and abandoned by a mammal, such as a hare or squirrel. She quickly raises one generation of worker bees. Then she lays special eggs, which will become queens, in the nest. The worker bees help her stock the nest with honey and pollen, and keep the nest warm by beating their wings.

A good nest is a real prize and is well worth fighting for. The two common bee species fight brutal battles over good nests. One emerges from its winter freeze first and builds its nest. Then the other species emerges, finds the first bee's nest, and tries to take it. A raging battle takes place, and the smaller queen dies. A queen that takes over the nest of another species also takes over the workers, forcing them to rear her eggs.

A Fly in the Nose

As you can see, conditions in the Arctic are hard, so insects must use whatever strategies are available to them in order to survive. Many become *parasites,* which means they live off other animals. Two types of flies have found that the caribou is a great place to live.

The *warble fly* lays its eggs in the caribou's thick hair. When the eggs hatch, the larvae penetrate the skin and make their way to the middle of the caribou's back. There they live just beneath the surface of the caribou's skin, making openings in order to breathe.

While this is going on "behind the caribou's back," the *botfly* is planning its strategy right in front of the caribou's nose! The botfly leaves its larvae in the nostrils of an unsuspecting caribou. It is warm enough inside the caribou's nose for the larvae to develop and grow there during the winter. During the spring, the flies drop to the ground, often after being sneezed out by the caribou.

7

Protecting the Pole

We like to imagine caribou rambling happily through the tundra, polar bears playing on the ice, and owls laying their eggs in untouched snow. But the truth is that caribou have to dodge oil pipelines, polar bears end up eating garbage, and owls lay their eggs in polluted snow. All arctic creatures have been affected by the presence of humanity. If we are not careful, we could destroy their homes—and their lives—completely.

A Pole in Danger?

It's not as hard to explore the Arctic now as it was for Robert Peary in 1909. Helicopters and snowmobiles make it easy to get around. They have also made it easier for the minerals, resources, and animals of the Arctic to fall into people's hands.

For years, whales and seals have been hunted. So have polar bears, walruses, caribou, and foxes. International agreements now give whales, seals, and polar bears some protection. The Inuit Eskimos are allowed to kill the animals they need in order to survive. But in general, the threat from hunting is no longer as serious as it once was. One new fear, however, is that walrus tusks will become more valuable now that laws have made elephant tusks very difficult to get.

The main threat to animals in the Arctic, however, is the loss and pollution of the land. One of the reasons this is such a serious threat is that the *ecosystem,* or environment, of the Arctic is a simple one. There are not that many plants and animals in the Arctic, so each one is very important in the food chain. Each species plays an important role, and any intrusion has great impact. Often, garbage left by tourists and scientists isn't *biodegradable,* or capable of being broken into simpler substances that do not damage the environment. Frozen tundra crushed by feet and tires does not spring back to life.

Even the air in the Arctic is in danger. Gases and particles from industrial plants in the lower regions of the Arctic Circle are carried through the air. During the winter, there is no wind or rain to wash them away. Eventually they fall to the ground in snow.

The Arctic also contains many resources that are important to people, such as copper, iron ore, gold, zinc, other metals, and natural gas. But the discovery of oil is one of the biggest issues involving the Arctic. The United States, Canada, Norway, and Greenland are all actively searching for oil in this region.

Companies drill for both oil and natural gas on the North Slope of Alaska. Oil is pumped down to Prudhoe Bay, in southern Alaska, through a pipeline that runs for almost 800 miles and can pump about 53 million gallons of oil per day. As with other industrial development, land is lost to factories, mines, roads, and people. Nature has been given some consideration by pipeline designers, however. Special sections were made in the pipeline so that herds of caribou could still cross during their annual migrations.

Oil exploration increases the risk of accidents. Alaska's Prince William Sound will never be the same since an oil tanker spilled nearly 11 million gallons of crude oil there in March 1989, destroying much of the wildlife.

Planning Ahead

Should all development of the Arctic be stopped? Or should the resources be retrieved at any cost? Should tourists be allowed into the remote areas of the Arctic? And what about the native people who find their land and survival at risk?

Both politicians and scientists are aware that these questions need to be tackled. In

1988, all the nations that fall within the arctic region formed an international group to study the Arctic. The group is called the International Arctic Science Committee, or IASC. Its goal is "to promote international cooperation and coordination of scientific research in the Arctic, for the benefit of peoples of the region and for the development of world scientific knowledge."

We can only hope that people will think very carefully before they act, so that year after year, polar bears and arctic squirrels will be able to emerge from their winter dens to greet a new spring as it blooms across their beautiful frozen land.

Lending a Hand

What can you do to help protect the Arctic? You can find out more about the Arctic—the animals, plants, and people who live there. See what you can learn from books in your library. Then write to these environmental groups for information. Show your support for their work to protect the arctic wildlife.

Defenders of Wildlife
1244 19th Street NW
Washington, DC
  20036

Greenpeace
1436 U Street NW
Washington, DC
  20009

Natural Resources
   Defense Council
40 West 20th Street
New York, NY 10011

World Wildlife Fund
1255 23rd Street NW
Washington, DC
20037

If you are especially concerned about pollution in the seas and oceans, write to:

The Center for Marine Conservation
1725 DeSales Street NW, Suite 500
Washington, DC 20036

Some people want to drill for oil and gas in Alaska, in an area that has so far been protected. It is called the Arctic National Wildlife Refuge. Environmentalists think drilling would endanger the animals that live there. To find out more, write to:

Sierra Club
730 Polk Street
San Francisco, CA 94109

Alaska is home to many national preserves and parks. If you want them to remain protected, show your support by writing to:

The National Park System
Department of the Interior
C Street NW
Washington, DC 20240